2083/0119

NOHANT-VIC NEAR LA CHATRE

Photograph by Walter H. Thomas, Philadelphia

ENVIRONS OF LOUVIERS, THE CHURCH OF PINTERVILLE

LA CHATRE—LA GRAND-FONT

VERNEUIL—OLD CHURCH, RUE DES MARRONIERS

Photos by Walter H. Thomas, Philadelphia

93

HONFLEUR—THE CHURCH OF SAINT-CATHERINE

Photograph by Walter H. Thomas, Philadelphia

ENVIRONS OF GAUDEBEC, CHURCH OF SAINT-NICOLAS

Photograph by Walter H. Thomas, Philadelphia

VIERZON—PLACE D'EGLISE

LISIEUX—TOWER OF THE XIV CENTURY

91

CHILLON—COURT AND STAIRS OF HONOR
Photograph by Walter H. Thomas, Philadelphia

ETRETAT, NORMANDY
Photograph by Walter H. Thomas, Philadelphia

OUILLY-LE-VICOMTE, CHURCH OF THE XIII CENTURY

IZÉ, BRITTANY, TOWN HALL

BOSC-GUERARD-SAINT-ADRIEN NEAR ROUEN

88

CHURCH AT NIVILLERS

DROUE—CHURCH OF THE XI CENTURY

SAINT-MARTIN DE LA LIEUE—X CENTURY

PETIT—QUEVILLY. CHURCH

86

LISIEUX—CHURCH OF OUILLY-LE-VICOMTE, X CENTURY

LA VIEUX-RUE, NEAR ROUEN

PONT-L'EVEQUE, CHURCH OF SAINT-MÉLAINE

85

SAINT-NICOLAS DE BLIQUETUIT

CLUNY, ANCIENT ABBEY

SENLIS—THE PRIORY SAINT MAURICE BUILT BY HENRY IV

SAINT ALBAN

BEUVREIL (NORMANDY) PORCH OF CHURCH

82

HONFLEUR—THE MARKET PLACE

Photograph by Edward B. Stratton, Boston

MORGNY NEAR ROUEN

NOTRE DAME DU THIL NEAR BEAUVAIS—CHURCH OF SAINT LUCIEN

MONTMAIN NEAR ROUEN—VILLAGE CHURCH

SAINT PIERRE DE MANNEVILLE—NEAR ROUEN

LISIEUX—CHATEAU DE BOUTTEMONT

MONT-SAINT-MICHEL

CLUNY—ANCIENT ABBEY

EVREUX—RUINS OF AN OLD MANOR

STE. ANDRESSE—NORMANDY—MANOIR DE VITANVAL

ORLEANS—HOUSE OF AGNES SOREL

STE. ANDRESSE—NORMANDY—MANOIR DE VITANVAL

ORLEANS—HOUSE OF AGNES SOREL

LOUVIERS—OLD HOUSE IN RUE HÔTEL DE VILLE

MONT-SAINT-MICHEL—STREET IN THE TOWN

LUYNES—THE CHATEAU

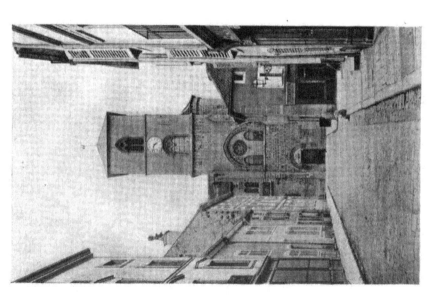

NEUFCHATEAU—STREET AND CHURCH OF SAINT-CHRISTOPHE

CONCHES—ANCIENT ABBEY OF THE BENEDICTINS

PENCRAN—MORGUE OF THE XVI CENTURY

CHATEAU DE MORVILLE

GACÉ—CHATEAU—WEST VIEW

CHAMPIGNÉ—CHATEAU DE LA HAMONIÈRE

ENVIRONS OF COMPIÈGNE—CHATEAU DE PIESSIS-BRION

CÔTES-DU-NORD—CHATEAU DE LA MOGLAIS

VAUBUIN—PAVILLON HENRY IV

GENNES (BRITTANY) THE CHATEAU DE LA MOTTE

ENVIRONS OF BAYEUX—RUINS OF THE CHATEAU D'ARGOUZES

LE-BREUIL EN AUGE—CHATEAU, XVI CENTURY

LISIEUX—THE CHATEAU HERMIVAL—XVI CENTURY

CHATEAU DE CAVIGNY—XVI CENTURY

SAINT-TOL-DE-LEON—HOUSE OF THE XVI CENTURY

CHAUMONT—INTERIOR COURT VIEW OF THE CHATEAU

NEAR AMBOISE—MANOIR D'ARISÉ

SARTHE—CHATEAU DE LA FLOTTE

CHATEAU DE COURTANGIS, NEAR LAMNAY

LOIR-ET-CHER—CHATEAU DE MOUSSEAUX

SAINT-JAMES—CHATEAU DE PALUELLE—XVI CENTURY

65

CHATELDON—THE CHATEAU

CHATEAU CHASTLAVA
Photo by Edward B. Stratton, Boston

AUNEAU—THE CHATEAU—NORTH VIEW

CHATEAU DE FOUGERES—COURT VIEW

LISIEUX—CHATEAU BREUIL-EN-ANGE

HUELGOAT, THE COURT OF CHATEAU DU RUSQUE

SAINT-PIERRE-SUR-DIVES—HOUSE OF THOMAS DUNOT, XVI CENTURY

LA CHAISE-DIEU—HOUSE OF THE XV CENTURY

RIOM—HOUSE RUE DE MOZAC

ROUEN—HOUSE, RUE DES ARPENTS

RIOM—HOUSE RUE DE MOZAC

ROUEN—HOUSE, RUE DES ARPENTS

LANGEAIS—THE HOUSE OF RABELAIS

VALENCE—THE CHATEAU DE BEAUREGARD

AVRANCHES—OLD BARRACKS

RAMBOUILLET—ENTRANCE TO NATIONAL FARM

TOURS—HOUSE RUE DU CYGNE

ABBEVILLE—OLD HOUSE

ANNOUVILLE—OLD HOUSE

GALLARDON—RUE LA GRANDE

ROUEN—HOUSE OF DIANA OF POITIERS

MONTOIRE—MAISON FAUBOURG SAINT OUSTRILLE

MONTOIRE—MAISON FAUBOURG SAINT OUSTRILLE

DOL—MAISONS DES PLAIDS, XV CENTURY

LAMBALLE—HOUSES OF THE XVI CENTURY

VERNEUIL—OLD HOUSE IN RUE DU CANON

PAIMPOL—ANCIENT ABBEY OF BEAUPORT

ANGERS—MAISON DE LA VOÛTE

51

VITRÉ—OLD HOUSES, RUE PUITS-PESÉ

50

ROUEN—RUE DES MATELAS

SAUMUR—OLD HOUSES, RUE DACIER

49

ROUEN—HOUSE OF THE XV CENTURY

ETAMPES—HOUSE OF ANNE DE PISSELEU

48

POITIERS—LOGIS DE LA GRANDE BARRE

47

TOURS—HOUSES ON PLACE FOIRE-LE-ROI

LE MANS—MAISON SCARRON

USSY (CALVADOS)—THE MANOR

LE MANS—MAISON SCARRON

USSY (CALVADOS)—THE MANOR

TULLE—RUE D'ALVERGE

45

BOURGES—HOUSE OF GUILLAUME PELVOYSIN

LUYNES (INDRE-ET-LOIRE) VILLAGE AND CHATEAU

LUYNES (INDRE-ET-LOIRE) VILLAGE STREET

SAINT-BRIEUX—HOUSES, RUE FARDEL

43

BEAUVAIS—HOUSE IN RUE SAINT LAURENT

ROSCOFF—HOUSE OF MARIE STUART

42

FARM AND MANOR HOUSES, CHATEAUX AND SMALL CHURCHES

VERNEUIL—HOUSE RUE DES TANNERIES

CHATENDUN—HOUSE RUE ST. LUBIN

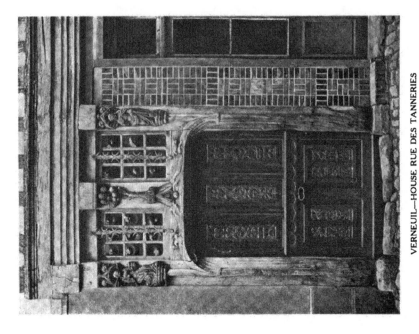

VERNEUIL—HOUSE RUE DES TANNERIES

41

CHATENDUN—HOUSE RUE ST. LUBIN

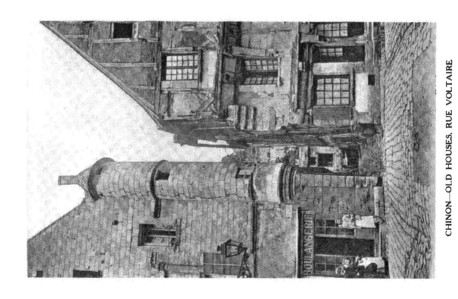

CHINON—OLD HOUSES, RUE VOLTAIRE

40

AURAY—RUE AU LAIT

ROUEN—HOUSE, RUE AMPÈRE

BLOIS—HOUSE OF THE XVI CENTURY

38

LAMBALLE—OLD HOUSE IN RUE BASSE

BLOIS—HOUSE OF THE XVI CENTURY

38

LAMBALLE—OLD HOUSE IN RUE BASSE.

TOURS—HOUSE OF JEAN GALLAND

37

MONTOIRE—HOUSE ON LA GRANDE PLACE

SAINT POL DE LÉON—MAISON CANONIALE

LUYNES—HOUSES ON PLACE DE L'EGLISE

LISIEUX—OLD HOUSES NEAR THE PONT DE CAEN

CAUDEBEC-EN-CAUX—OLD HOUSES

LISIEUX—ROOM IN HOUSE IN RUE AUX FÉVRES
34

GALLARDON—HOUSE IN RUE LA GRANDE

ALBI—HÔTEL DE REYNES

33

ORLEANS—CORRIDOR IN THE HOUSE OF AGNES SOREL

VENDOME—CITY HALL

32

ARCHELLES—NORMANDY—MANOR HOUSE—FRONT VIEW

ARCHELLES—NORMANDY—MANOR HOUSE—SIDE VIEW

LOCHES—MAISONS DU CENTAURE ET LA CHANCELLERIE

AZAY-LE-RIDEAU—HOUSE BUILT IN 1442

ORBEC—HOTEL DE L'EQUERRE

29

BEAUNE—HÔTEL DE LA MARE—INTERIOR COURT

LISIEUX—MANOIR CARRÉ

27

LE VIEUX MANS—HOUSE IN RUE SAINTE-ANNE

ST. REMY-LA-VARENNE—THE PRIORY

CUNAULT—HOUSE OF THE XVI CENTURY

26

REIMS—HOTEL DE NICOLAS LE VERGEUR

BOURGES—HOTEL LALLEMANT

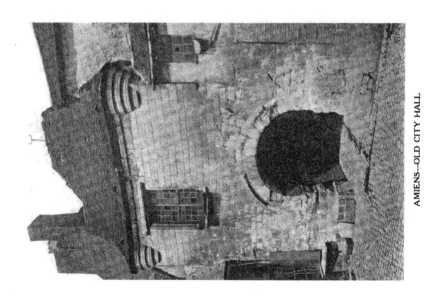

AMIENS—OLD CITY HALL

24

MONT SAINT MICHEL—COUR DE LA MERVEILLE

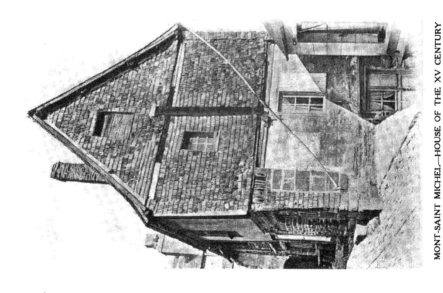

MONT-SAINT MICHEL—HOUSE OF THE XV CENTURY

23

TOURS—OLD HOUSES IN RUE DU CHANGE

LANGRES—HOUSE IN RUE DU CARDINAL MORLOT

22

BOURGES—OLD HOUSE IN RUE BLANCHE

21

LISIEUX—OLD HOUSE IN RUE D'ORBEC

LISIEUX—HOUSE OF THE XV CENTURY

MOULINS—HOUSE OF THE XV CENTURY

20

LOUVIERS—HOUSE OF THE XV CENTURY

VANNES—HOUSES OF THE XV CENTURY

MARTINVILLE—OLD HOUSES

18

CAUDEBEC—OLD HOUSES IN RUE CORDONNERIE

CAHORS—HOUSE OF THE XVI CENTURY

17

LE MANS—HOUSE OF THE XVI CENTURY

CHENONCEAUX—CHURCH AND HOUSE OF THE PAGES OF FRANCIS I

DOL—OLD HOUSES IN LA GRANDE RUE

VIERZON, OLD HOUSES IN RUE DU CHAMP COMMUNE

PONT-L'EVEQUE, NORMANDY—OLD HOUSE

LA CHATRE—OLD GOTHIC WELL

14

ENVIRONS OF CONCARNEAU—AN OLD MILL

FARM HOUSE IN NORMANDY

Photograph by Walter H. Thomas, Philadelphia.

FARM HOUSE IN NORMANDY

Photograph by Walter H. Thomas, Philadelphia.

13

TOUQUES (CALVADOS), THE MARKET, XV CENTURY

NEAR MONT-SAINT-MICHEL—VILLAGE STREET

LAMBALLE—MAISON À TOURELLE

USSY—ENTRANCE TO THE FARM DU POT

11

CHAUMONT-SUR-LOIRE—THE STABLES

RAMBOUILLET—THE DOG KENNEL

NEAR AUTUN—FARM BUILDINGS BELONGING TO THE CHATEAU DE MONTJEU

SAMOIS—OLD HOUSES NEAR THE COURT HOUSE

9

ST. JAQUES—NEAR LISIEUX—OLD NORMAN FARM HOUSE

LE VIEUX MANS—MAISON À VOUTE

BORDS DE LA RANCE—A FARM IN BRITTANY

SAINT-JULIEN-DU-SAULT—OLD HOUSE

CHATEAU DE GRATOT—THE FARM

NORMANDY—FERME LA VALLAUINE

NORMANDY—MANOIR D'ANGO

NORMANDY—MANOIR D'ANGO

NORMANDY—MANOIR D'ANGO

NORMANDY—MANOIR D'ANGO

NORMANDY—FERME DE TURPE

NORMANDY—FERME DE TURPE

VITRÉ—HOUSES IN RUE BALAŹE

ENVIRONS OF LOUVIERS—VILLAGE SMITHY

VITRÉ—HOUSES IN RUE BALAŹE

ENVIRONS OF LOUVIERS—VILLAGE SMITHY

NEAR BEAUMONT LE ROGER, NORMANDY

NEAR BEAUMONT LE ROGER, NORMANDY

Photos by Walter H. Thomas, Philadelphia.

1

FARM AND MANOR HOUSES, CHATEAUX AND SMALL CHURCHES

NEAR BEAUMONT LE ROGER, NORMANDY

NEAR BEAUMONT LE ROGER, NORMANDY

Photos by Walter H. Thomas, Philadelphia.

1

From the XI century to the XVII it would appear that no one could build unbeautifully if he tried: at all events he did not, and every farm, cottage, chapel, village church is of a beauty we cannot touch today no matter how great our erudition and how conscientious the pains we take with our task. It is well sometimes to contrast what is left us in some little French or Italian or English town, with any New England village that has been touched by "prosperity," or some thriving town of the Middle West. Compare the half-timbered or tiled and plastered cottages, the modest villa or manor or chateau, the carved shop fronts, the parish church with its remains of old handiwork, the very streets and door yards and gardens, with the bold-faced "mansions" of the prosperous, the bald, raw dwellings of the 'seventies, the Noah's Ark "meeting houses" and the awesome "Gothic" of the more advanced religious societies, the Carnegie Library, the brick stores and the rows of slate-coloured tenements. In the first instance we are dealing with remnants of a world five centuries ago, a world not infrequently referred to in journalism as the "Dark Ages." In the second we have before us the visible expression of a Modern Civilization that after a century of headlong advances has at last reached its perfect consummation. What does it all mean? It is not an accident, a negligible episode, a consideration of no importance; it has a deep and vital significance and one that it is our task to discover. This beauty that clothes these old buildings with imperishable glory—the little equally with the great —is a real thing with a real meaning behind. Perhaps now, when the thing that expressed itself in universal ugliness, is revealing something of its actual nature, we shall be prompted to look backward to and through the recorded beauty of old days, to see if there we may not find something besides that beauty itself—the mystery of the great force and the forgotten system that made this universal beauty not only possible but unescapable.

RALPH ADAMS CRAM.

for the architect, and doubly so for the student of architecture. These little churches and chateaux and farm-houses are priceless documents in the recording of the most universal and popular type of architecture the world has known, but they are as well invaluable for the architect himself, since nine tenths of what he does must be conceived in the same scale and of similar dimensions. One may find all over the country, innumerable churches, supposedly Gothic, and one hundred feet long, or even less, which have been laboriously worked out from the pictures of the vast five hundred foot cathedrals of France and England, with results that can better be imagined than described. There is one in particular I have in mind, in a provincial town in one of our Eastern States, which is certainly not over 90 feet in length, and is simply a parody of the cathedral of Notre Dame in Paris. It is, I think, Baptist (or possibly Congregational) and it is built of yellow brick with brown-stone "trimmings." France can show two hundred churches of similar dimensions, conceived in a scale fitting their dimensions, any one of which might have served as a better model, but an insane passion for bigness of model and a lack of available documents in the shape of pictures has led to this sad but humorous aberration that might otherwise have been avoided, to the credit of architecture and the edification of the general public.

Another case is a certain "Tudor Gothic," Episcopalian church where the original length of 250 feet has been cut in half, and the height reduced in proportion. Everything is minimized in the same way, except the detail, mouldings, carving, sculptures, and these remain of the same scale as in the original.

Of course all this sort of thing is grossly unintelligent, but we shall never get away from it until we can take for our necessary models, work of the same type and scale as the problem we ourselves have to solve. It is a good sign that many of the books now being brought out deal exclusively with work of human scale and common nature, while the "Cathedral books" are being relegated to the place where they belong—a place of dignity and importance, but one that deals with inspiration rather than with precept.

As we look at these inconspicuous works of "unpremeditated art," we must be impressed with the unfailing beauty that marks them all.

IV

styles that have this title have achieved a bad name through the too exclusive dependence by their expositors on the great monuments, that are only too often manifestations of a singular barbarism. These were the self-conscious products of arrogance and bad taste, official in status and wholly sundered from society as a whole. If we turn from the villas of Paladio and the churches of San Gallo and the palaces of Sansovino to the farms and villini and convents and little chapels scattered broadcast over the South we come back at once to the human scale, and to a native good taste that refuses to be browbeaten by insolent pride and magisterial competence.

In the case of Medieval architecture there was complete identity of motive and of standards between the great work and the small, but in much of the latter may be found local and special qualities that do not occur elsewhere and are invaluable for the estimating of the art as a whole. When the Renaissance came in it first assailed the great, or official buildings—abbeys, cathedrals, palaces,—and even when it had completely established itself there it still failed for a long time to influence the minor work to any material degree. Long after the nobles and the great ecclesiastics were building themselves their vast erections in the most approved Classical taste, the parish clergy and small lords and prosperous burgers, true to their adherence to the old and fast dissolving ways and standards, continued to build more or less as their fathers before them. As the classical influence slowly worked its way here it was curiously transmuted by popular taste, and showed itself in quaint and engaging guise, penetrating the Gothic shell, transforming it in very fascinating ways, and still leaving it rather of the old order than of the new.

This is true not only of France, but of Spain, Flanders, the Rhineland, and particularly of England, where some of the old traditions of Medievalism maintained themselves well into the XIX century, and in those parts of the country furthest removed from the Court and the great new centres of trade and industry.

Since, therefore, there is so much of the real art of the people to be found in the generally ignored buildings of the end of the Middle Ages and the earlier part of the Renaissance, a book such as this, which confines itself to precisely this sort of thing, is very valuable

its existence, wherein this new and free system reached its full development, and when it extended itself throughout all Western Europe. The Renaissance is the time that marks the first assault on the well established scheme of life, and the years that follow, even to our own day, form that space of time wherein the "Christian Commonwealth" was beaten down and at last a close approach recorded to the servile state of antiquity.

From the first beginnings of the Middle Ages in the last quarter of the X century, the "grand style" in architecture develops side by side with the minor style, as, under the new social conditions, must have been the case. Great abbeys, cathedrals, castles, reveal themselves, growing ever more complex and gigantic, but art is no longer the possession of a favoured few, it is now the heritage of all, and for one great monument there are scores of little churches, minor priories, small castles, with somewhat later, town houses, chapels, farms, manors and chateaux in ever-increasing numbers and infallible charm. To build up a philosophy of Medieval art and a science of Gothic architecture on the foundations of only such structures as the abbeys of Caen, the cathedrals of Chartres, Notre Dame, Rheims, Amiens, Beauvais, to the total ignoring of the work and the people as a whole, is absurd, for the art of Medievalism was essentially a communal art and to a degree never approached before. It was not the product of a few highly trained specialists expressing their own idiosyncracies, but the spontaneous and instinctive art of a whole people, or rather of groups of people acting under a common impulse, in accordance with varying conditions, to a common end.

For this reason it is impossible to form an adequate idea of Medieval art until full regard is given to the modest products of minor scale; such, for example, as those illustrated in this volume. Fortunately, this is still possible; it is true that myriads of priceless examples have been swept away through accident, war, revolution, ignorance, bad taste, but the original number was so great that in spite of all, enough remain to afford a fair idea of what the style was in itself, and as well of the extraordinary beauty that must have clothed the Middle Ages as with a garment.

The same is true of the Renaissance and after: the architectural

PREFACE

AS, DURING the last century, the "human scale" vanished from life and a kind of brutal imperialism took its place to poison and finally destroy the whole system of human associations left over from better times, so our standards of architectural judgment were transformed, becoming at last as degenerate as our architectural style was debased. Our whole system of architectural philosophy, architectural teaching, and architectural determinism, so dogmatic and secure, is a thing of mushroom growth; a century has seen it come into existence, though the first premonitory symptoms are revealed during the beginnings of the Renaissance. Under this system not only has the "grand manner" held as a standard of judgment as between one historic style and another, and in the controlling of all scholastic design, but its imperialistic scale has been applied to the determining of architectural philosophy and history to such an extent that a purely fictitious theory has been built up only on the basis of the "big things," to the total exclusion of the great mass of small work, whatever its period or its nationality.

It is probably true that the oldest styles—Egyptian, Greek, Roman, Byzantine—were styles of "big things," for until the Middle Ages freedom and an approximate democracy were unknown, the basis of Antiquity having been slavery. Therefore, whatever architecture there was, was official, whether secular or spiritual, and beyond the palace and the fortress on the one hand, the temple or church on the other, there was little of very great significance. It is rational enough, perhaps, to determine these styles on the basis of their magnificent ruins, or the records thereof, but with the advent of Medievalism, the status of society is changed and the method no longer applies.

The Medieval epoch was that period wherein was achieved for the first time a true democracy, under the only control that can insure

I

FARM HOUSES, MANOR HOUSES, MINOR CHATEAUX AND SMALL CHURCHES FROM THE ELEVENTH TO THE SIXTEENTH CENTURIES IN NORMANDY, BRITTANY AND OTHER PARTS OF FRANCE

With a Preface by

RALPH ADAMS CRAM, Litt. D., LL.D.

Fellow of the American Institute of Architects
Fellow of the Royal Geographical Society, Etc.

THE ARCHITECTURAL BOOK PUBLISHING COMPANY
PAUL WENZEL AND MAURICE KRAKOW
THIRTY-ONE EAST TWELFTH STREET, NEW YORK

IN NORMANDY

Lightning Source UK Ltd.
Milton Keynes UK
UKHW010818160223
417016UK00005B/108